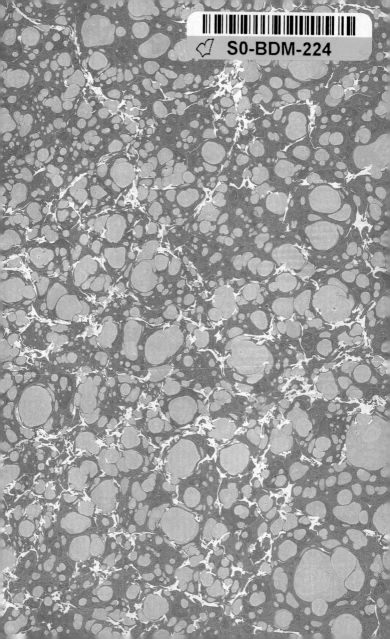

GREAT AMERICAN POETS

GREAT AMERICAN POETS

Henry Wadsworth Longfellow

❊❈❊❈❊❈❊❈❊❈❊❈❊❈❊❈❊❈❊❈❊❈❊❈❊❈❊❈❊❈❊❈❊

Edited and with an introduction
by Geoffrey Moore

 Clarkson N. Potter, Inc./Publishers NEW YORK

Published in the United States by Clarkson N. Potter, Inc.,
201 East 50th Street, New York, New York 10022
and distributed by Crown Publishers, Inc.
Published in Great Britain by Aurum Press Ltd.,
33 Museum Street, London WC1A 1LD.

CLARKSON N. POTTER, POTTER, THE GREAT POETS,
and colophon are trademarks of Clarkson N. Potter, Inc.

Picture research by Juliet Brightmore

Manufactured in Hong Kong

Library of Congress Cataloging-in-Publication Data

Longfellow, Henry Wadsworth. 1807–1882.
[Poems. Selections]
Henry Wadsworth Longfellow/edited and with an introduction by
Geoffrey Moore.
p.   cm. — (Great American poets)
ISBN 0–517–57380–6 : $8.95
I. Moore, Geoffrey.   II. Title.   III. Series.
PS2253.M5   1989
811'.3—DC20   89-4039
CIP
10   9   8   7   6   5   4   3   2   1
First American Edition

CONTENTS

INTRODUCTION

Of all the American poets in the nineteenth century, Longfellow was the most popular, for although he did not, like Walt Whitman or Emily Dickinson, forge for himself an unmistakably original style, he expressed with great felicity the feelings of what Dr Johnson called 'the common reader'.

What *was* original about Longfellow's contribution to literature was the degree to which he plunged into verse experiment. In *Hiawatha*, for example, he used the running rhythm of the Finnish *Kalevala*, thus capturing perfectly the fleetfoot, moccasined sound which he wanted for his Indian braves. If his poetry sometimes seems a little thin compared with the lush verbiage of the English Victorian poets, this is partly because he was subject to pressures which the English never knew – the pressure of American primness, for example, which made him a 'schoolroom poet'.

Longfellow became by adoption a member of what James Russell Lowell called the 'inoffensive, untitled aristocracy' of New England, very much in the 'paleface' tradition, as defined by Philip Rahv in his famous essay *Paleface and Redskin*. Where he is at his best is in the clear honesty of 'Mezzo Cammin' and the empathy of 'Chaucer'.

His contemporaries, however, admired him most for the memorability of such poems as 'The Arrow and the Song' and 'The Tide Rises, The Tide Falls'. Indeed, for his musical quality the only other American poet who vies with him is Poe. Unlike Longfellow, however, Poe worked by theory and effect – which was why he appealed so much to the late nineteenth-century French

poets. There was no morality about Poe; Longfellow was all morality.

To see today the beautiful white clapboard house in Cambridge, Massachusetts, in which Longfellow lived is to get some idea of the man himself. True, the Craigie House had been built a hundred years earlier and was once Washington's headquarters, but this makes the point even more strongly. In the calmness and serenity which he achieved in later life – qualities which 'In the Churchyard at Cambridge' conveys so well – Longfellow retained, as I. A. Richards pointed out, something of the meditativeness of the eighteenth century.

That, at least, was one half of his persona; the other was that of the nineteenth-century story-teller. He could spin a tale in verse as effectively as any fiction writer – more effectively perhaps, since the nineteenth-century reader had none of the twentieth-century's aversion to poetry. It was possible, in fact, to have a bestseller in verse, and Longfellow did, being one of the very few Professors of Literature to accomplish such a feat.

His first professorship came when he was very young – only twenty-two, in fact. That was at his own College of Bowdoin in Maine where Nathaniel Hawthorne had been a fellow student. This Chair of Romance Languages included provision for extensive foreign travel and in the next two years Longfellow travelled widely in Europe. His reward for excellent academic work was the offer of the Smith Professorship at Harvard, which came before he was thirty.

When Longfellow was in his late thirties and early forties there began appearing those stories in verse which made him so popular with the general public:

The Belfry of Bruges in 1846, *Evangeline* in 1847 and *Kavanaugh: a Tale* in 1849. *The Courtship of Miles Standish* brought the Puritan period to life, but undoubtedly Longfellow's greatest success was *Hiawatha* in 1858. He had done his research and, like Fenimore Cooper, he felt deeply for the values with which he imbued his Noble Savage. The fact that *Hiawatha* is still popular today wherever English is spoken gives us some indication of the extraordinary qualities of this 'down-Easter' from Portland, Maine.

Longfellow's father may have been a judge and a member of Congress, but the family was provincial. Yet this provincial boy conquered the English-speaking world through his verse and earned himself a place in that holy of holies, Westminster Abbey. Life was no empty dream for Longfellow; he, of all people, left footprints on the sands of time.

Inevitably, a comparison with Tennyson comes to mind, for they were contemporaries and served much the same public. They were both didactic and worked within the public morality of their day; they were both superb craftsmen; and each had his own peculiar melodic appeal. Yet with Tennyson the reader may feel sometimes, as W. H. Auden pointed out, 'Yes, very effective, but does he believe what he is saying?' With Longfellow we cannot avoid the impression of utter sincerity. His very popularity inspired him, not with cynicism, but with a sense of mission. It is this that is his most American characteristic.

GEOFFREY MOORE

The Wreck of the Hesperus

It was the schooner Hesperus,
    That sailed the wintry sea;
And the skipper had taken his little daughter,
    To bear him company.

Blue were her eyes as the fairy-flax,
    Her cheeks like the dawn of day,
And her bosom white as the hawthorn buds
    That ope in the month of May.

The skipper he stood beside the helm,
    His pipe was in his mouth,
And he watched how the veering flaw did blow
    The smoke now West, now South.

Then up and spake an old Sailòr,
    Had sailed the Spanish Main,
'I pray thee, put into yonder port,
    For I fear a hurricane.

Last night the moon had a golden ring,
    And to-night no moon we see!'
The skipper he blew a whiff from his pipe,
    And a scornful laugh laughed he.

Colder and louder blew the wind,
    A gale from the North-east,
The snow fell hissing in the brine,
    And the billows frothed like yeast.

Down came the storm, and smote amain
    The vessel in its strength;
She shuddered and paused, like a frighted steed,
    Then leaped her cable's length.

'Come hither! come hither! my little daughter,
    And do not tremble so;
For I can weather the roughest gale
    That ever wind did blow.'

He wrapped her warm in his seaman's coat
    Against the stinging blast;
He cut a rope from a broken spar,
    And bound her to the mast.

'O father! I hear the church-bells ring,
    O say, what may it be?'
'Tis a fog-bell on a rock-bound coast!' –
    And he steered for the open sea.

'O father! I hear the sound of guns,
    O say, what may it be?'
'Some ship in distress, that cannot live
    In such an angry sea!'

'O father! I see a gleaming light,
    O say, what may it be?'
But the father answered never a word,
    A frozen corpse was he.

Lashed to the helm, all stiff and stark,
    With his face turned to the skies,
The lantern gleamed through the gleaming snow
    On his fixed and glassy eyes.

Then the maiden clasped her hands and prayed
    That savèd she might be;
And she thought of Christ, who stilled the wave
    On the Lake of Galilee.

And fast through the midnight dark and drear,
    Through the whistling sleet and snow,
Like a sheeted ghost the vessel swept
    Towards the reef of Norman's Woe.

And ever the fitful gusts between
    A sound came from the land;
It was the sound of the trampling surf
    On the rocks and the hard sea-sand.

The breakers were right beneath her bows,
    She drifted a dreary wreck,
And a whooping billow swept the crew
    Like icicles from her deck.

She struck where the white and fleecy waves
    Looked soft as carded wool,
But the cruel rocks they gored her side
    Like the horns of an angry bull.

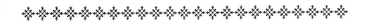

Her rattling shrouds, all sheathed in ice,
  With the masts went by the board;
Like a vessel of glass she stove and sank, –
  Ho! ho! the breakers roared!

At daybreak on the bleak sea-beach
  A fisherman stood aghast,
To see the form of a maiden fair
  Lashed close to a drifting mast.

The salt sea was frozen on her breast,
  The salt tears in her eyes;
And he saw her hair, like the brown sea-weed,
  On the billows fall and rise.

Such was the wreck of the Hesperus,
  In the midnight and the snow!
Christ save us all from a death like this,
  On the reef of Norman's Woe!

The Village Blacksmith

Under a spreading chestnut-tree
  The village smithy stands;
The smith, a mighty man is he,
  With large and sinewy hands;
And the muscles of his brawny arms
  Are strong as iron bands.

His hair is crisp, and black, and long;
  His face is like the tan;
His brow is wet with honest sweat,
  He earns whate'er he can,
And looks the whole world in the face,
  For he owes not any man.

Week in, week out, from morn till night,
  You can hear his bellows blow;
You can hear him swing his heavy sledge,
  With measured beat and slow,
Like a sexton ringing the village bell,
  When the evening sun is low.

And children coming home from school
  Look in at the open door;
They love to see the flaming forge,
  And hear the bellows roar,
And catch the burning sparks that fly
  Like chaff from a threshing-floor.

He goes on Sunday to the church,
    And sits among his boys;
He hears the parson pray and preach,
    He hears his daughter's voice
Singing in the village choir,
    And it makes his heart rejoice.

It sounds to him like her mother's voice
    Singing in Paradise!
He needs must think of her once more,
    How in the grave she lies;
And with his hard, rough hand he wipes
    A tear out of his eyes.

Toiling, – rejoicing, – sorrowing,
    Onward through life he goes;
Each morning sees some task begin,
    Each evening sees it close;
Something attempted, something done,
    Has earned a night's repose.

Thanks, thanks to thee, my worthy friend,
    For the lesson thou hast taught!
Thus at the flaming forge of life
    Our fortunes must be wrought;
Thus on its sounding anvil shaped
    Each burning deed and thought.

Excelsior

The shades of night were falling fast,
As through an Alpine village passed
A youth, who bore, 'mid snow and ice,
A banner with the strange device,
      Excelsior!

His brow was sad; his eye beneath
Flashed like a falchion from its sheath,
And like a silver clarion rung
The accents of that unknown tongue,
      Excelsior!

In happy homes he saw the light
Of household fires gleam warm and bright;
Above, the spectral glaciers shone,
And from his lips escaped a groan,
      Excelsior!

'Try not the Pass!' the old man said;
'Dark lowers the tempest overhead,
The roaring torrent is deep and wide!'
And loud that clarion voice replied,
      Excelsior!

'O stay,' the maiden said, 'and rest
Thy weary head upon this breast!'
A tear stood in his bright blue eye,
But still he answered, with a sigh,
      Excelsior!

'Beware the pine-tree's withered branch!
Beware the awful avalanche!'
This was the peasant's last Goodnight.
A voice replied, far up the height,
     Excelsior!

At break of day, as heavenward
The pious monks of Saint Bernard
Uttered the oft-repeated prayer,
A voice cried through the startled air,
     Excelsior!

A traveller, by the faithful hound,
Half-buried in the snow was found,
Still grasping in his hand of ice
That banner with the strange device,
     Excelsior!

There in the twilight cold and gray,
Lifeless, but beautiful, he lay,
And from the sky, serene and far,
A voice fell, like a falling star,
     Excelsior!

Mezzo Cammin

WRITTEN AT BOPPARD, ON THE RHINE,
AUGUST 25, 1842,
JUST BEFORE LEAVING FOR HOME.

Half of my life is gone, and I have let
   The years slip from me and have not fulfilled
   The aspiration of my youth, to build
   Some tower of song with lofty parapet.
Not indolence, nor pleasure, nor the fret
   Of restless passions that would not be stilled,
   But sorrow, and a care that almost killed,
   Kept me from what I may accomplish yet;
Though, half-way up the hill, I see the Past
   Lying beneath me with its sounds and sights, –
   A city in the twilight dim and vast,
With smoking roofs, soft bells, and gleaming lights, –
   And hear above me on the autumnal blast
   The cataract of Death far thundering from the heights.

The Slave's Dream

Beside the ungathered rice he lay,
　　His sickle in his hand;
His breast was bare, his matted hair
　　Was buried in the sand.
Again, in the mist and shadow of sleep,
　　He saw his Native Land.

Wide through the landscape of his dreams
　　The lordly Niger flowed;
Beneath the palm-trees on the plain
　　Once more a king he strode;
And heard the tinkling caravans
　　Descend the mountain-road.

He saw once more his dark-eyed queen
　　Among her children stand;
They clasped his neck, they kissed his cheeks,
　　They held him by the hand! –
A tear burst from the sleeper's lids
　　And fell into the sand.

And then at furious speed he rode
　　Along the Niger's bank;
His bridle-reins were golden chains,
　　And, with a martial clank,
At each leap he could feel his scabbard of steel
　　Smiting his stallion's flank.

Before him, like a blood-red flag,
    The bright flamingoes flew;
From morn till night he followed their flight,
    O'er plains where the tamarind grew,
Till he saw the roofs of Caffre huts,
    And the ocean rose to view.

At night he heard the lion roar,
    And the hyena scream,
And the river-horse, as he crushed the reeds
    Beside some hidden stream;
And it passed, like a glorious roll of drums,
    Through the triumph of his dream.

The forests, with their myriad tongues,
    Shouted of liberty;
And the Blast of the Desert cried aloud,
    With a voice so wild and free,
That he started in his sleep and smiled
    At their tempestuous glee.

He did not feel the driver's whip,
    Nor the burning heat of day;
For Death had illumined the Land of Sleep,
    And his lifeless body lay
A worn-out fetter, that the soul
    Had broken and thrown away!

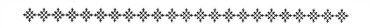

Seaweed

When descends on the Atlantic
        The gigantic
Storm-wind of the equinox,
Landward in his wrath he scourges
        The toiling surges,
Laden with seaweed from the rocks:

From Bermuda's reefs; from edges
        Of sunken ledges,
In some far-off, bright Azore;
From Bahama, and the dashing,
        Silver-flashing
Surges of San Salvador;

From the tumbling surf, that buries
        The Orkneyan skerries,
Answering the hoarse Hebrides;
And from wrecks of ships, and drifting
        Spars, uplifting
On the desolate, rainy seas; –

Ever drifting, drifting, drifting
    On the shifting
Currents of the restless main;
Till in sheltered coves, and reaches
    Of sandy beaches,
All have found repose again.

So when storms of wild emotion
    Strike the ocean
Of the poet's soul, ere long
From each cave and rocky fastness,
    In its vastness,
Floats some fragment of a song:

From the far-off isles enchanted,
    Heaven has planted
With the golden fruit of Truth;
From the flashing surf, whose vision
    Gleams Elysian
In the tropic clime of Youth;

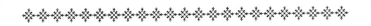

From the strong Will, and the Endeavour
     That for ever
Wrestle with the tides of Fate;
From the wreck of Hopes far-scattered,
     Tempest-shattered,
Floating waste and desolate; –

Ever drifting, drifting, drifting
     On the shifting
Currents of the restless heart;
Till at length in books recorded,
     They, like hoarded
Household words, no more depart.

The Day is Done

The day is done, and the darkness
    Falls from the wings of Night,
As a feather is wafted downward
    From an eagle in his flight.

I see the lights of the village
    Gleam through the rain and the mist,
And a feeling of sadness comes o'er me
    That my soul cannot resist:

A feeling of sadness and longing,
    That is not akin to pain.
And resembles sorrow only
    As the mist resembles the rain.

Come, read to me some poem,
    Some simple and heartfelt lay,
That shall soothe this restless feeling,
    And banish the thoughts of day.

Not from the grand old masters,
    Not from the bards sublime,
Whose distant footsteps echo
    Through the corridors of Time.

For, like strains of martial music,
    Their mighty thoughts suggest
Life's endless toil and endeavour;
    And to-night I long for rest.

Read from some humbler poet,
    Whose songs gushed from his heart,
As showers from the clouds of summer,
    Or tears from the eyelids start;

Who, through long days of labour,
    And nights devoid of ease,
Still heard in his soul the music
    Of wonderful melodies.

Such songs have power to quiet
   The restless pulse of care,
And come like the benediction
   That follows after prayer.

Then read from the treasured volume
   The poem of thy choice,
And lend to the rhyme of the poet
   The beauty of thy voice.

And the night shall be filled with music,
   And the cares that infest the day
Shall fold their tents, like the Arabs,
   And as silently steal away.

The Arrow and the Song

I shot an arrow into the air,
It fell to earth, I knew not where;
For, so swiftly it flew, the sight
Could not follow it in its flight.

I breathed a song into the air,
It fell to earth, I knew not where;
For who has sight so keen and strong
That it can follow the flight of song?

Long, long afterward, in an oak
I found the arrow, still unbroke;
And the song, from beginning to end,
I found again in the heart of a friend.

Hiawatha's Departure

By the shore of Gitche Gumee,
By the shining Big-Sea-Water,
At the doorway of his wigwam,
In the pleasant Summer morning,
Hiawatha stood and waited.
　All the air was full of freshness,
All the earth was bright and joyous,
And before him, through the sunshine,
Westward toward the neighbouring forest
Passed in golden swarms the Ahmo,
Passed the bees, the honey-makers,
Burning, singing in the sunshine.
　Bright above him shone the heavens,
Level spread the lake before him;
From its bosom leaped the sturgeon,
Sparkling, flashing in the sunshine;
On its margin the great forest
Stood reflected in the water,
Every tree-top had its shadow,
Motionless beneath the water.
　From the brow of Hiawatha
Gone was every trace of sorrow,
As the fog from off the water,
As the mist from off the meadow.
With a smile of joy and triumph,
With a look of exultation,
As of one who in a vision

Sees what is to be, but is not,
Stood and waited Hiawatha.
    Toward the sun his hands were lifted,
Both the palms spread out against it,
And between the parted fingers
Fell the sunshine on his features,
Flecked with light his naked shoulders,
As it falls and flecks an oak-tree
Through the rifted leaves and branches.
    O'er the water floating, flying,
Something in the hazy distance,
Something in the mists of morning,
Loomed and lifted from the water,
Now seemed floating, now seemed flying,
Coming nearer, nearer, nearer.
    Was it Shingebis the diver?
Or the pelican, the Shada?
Or the heron, the Shuh-shuh-gah?
Or the white goose, Waw-be-wawa,
With the water dripping, flashing,
From its glossy neck and feathers?
    It was neither goose nor diver,
Neither pelican nor heron,
O'er the water floating, flying,
Through the shining mist of morning,
But a birch-canoe with paddles,
Rising, sinking on the water,
Dripping, flashing in the sunshine;
And within it came a people
From the distant land of Wabun,

From the farthest realms of morning
Came the Black-Robe chief, the Prophet,
He the Priest of Prayer, the Pale-face,
With his guides and his companions.
　And the noble Hiawatha,
With his hands aloft extended,
Held aloft in sign of welcome,
Waited, full of exultation
Till the birch-canoe with paddles
Grated on the shining pebbles,
Stranded on the sandy margin,
Till the Black-Robe chief, the Pale-face,
With the cross upon his bosom,
Landed on the sandy margin.
　Then the joyous Hiawatha
Cried aloud and spake in this wise:
'Beautiful is the sun, O strangers,
When you come so far to see us!
All our town in peace awaits you,
All our doors stand open for you;
You shall enter all our wigwams,
For the heart's right hand we give you.
　'Never bloomed the earth so gaily,
Never shone the sun so brightly,
As to-day they shine and blossom
When you come so far to see us!
Never was our lake so tranquil,
Nor so free from rocks and sand-bars;
For your birch-canoe in passing
Has removed both rock and sand-bar.

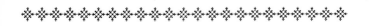

'Never before had our tobacco
Such a sweet and pleasant flavour,
Never the broad leaves of our cornfields
Were so beautiful to look on,
As they seem to us this morning,
When you come so far to see us!'
      And the Black-Robe chief made answer,
Stammered in his speech a little,
Speaking words yet unfamiliar:
'Peace be with you, Hiawatha,
Peace be with you and your people,
Peace of prayer, and peace of pardon,
Peace of Christ, and joy of Mary!'
      Then the generous Hiawatha
Led the strangers to his wigwam,
Seated them on skins of bison,
Seated them on skins of ermine,
And the careful, old Nokomis
Brought them food in bowls of bass-wood,
Water brought in birchen dippers,
And the calumet, the peace-pipe,
Filled and lighted for their smoking.
      All the old men of the village,
All the warriors of the nation,
All the Jossakeeds, the prophets,
The magicians, the Wabenos,
And the medicine-men, the Medas,
Came to bid the strangers welcome;
'It is well,' they said, 'O brothers,
That you come so far to see us!'

In a circle round the doorway,
With their pipes they sat in silence,
Waiting to behold the strangers,
Waiting to receive their message;
Till the Black-Robe chief, the Pale-face,
From the wigwam came to greet them,
Stammering in his speech a little,
Speaking words yet unfamiliar;
'It is well,' they said, 'O brother,
That you come so far to see us!'

Then the Black-Robe chief, the prophet,
Told his message to the people,
Told the purport of his mission,
Told them of the Virgin Mary,
And her blessed Son, the Saviour,
How in distant lands and ages
He had lived on earth as we do;
How he fasted, prayed and laboured;
How the Jews, the tribe accursed,
Mocked him, scourged him, crucified him;
How he rose from where they laid him,
Walked again with his disciples,
And ascended into heaven.

And the chiefs made answer, saying:
'We have listened to your message,
We have heard your words of wisdom,
We will think on what you tell us.
It is well for us, O brothers,
That you come so far to see us!'

Then they rose up and departed
Each one homeward to his wigwam,
To the young men and the women,
Told the story of the strangers
Whom the Master of Life had sent them
From the shining land of Wabun.

Heavy with the heat and silence
Grew the afternoon of Summer;
With a drowsy sound the forest
Whispered round the sultry wigwam,
With a sound of sleep the water
Rippled on the beach below it;
From the cornfields shrill and ceaseless
Sang the grasshopper, Pah-puk-keena;
And the guests of Hiawatha,
Weary with the heat of Summer,
Slumbered in the sultry wigwam.

Slowly o'er the simmering landscape
Fell the evening's dusk and coolness,
And the long and level sunbeams
Shot their spears into the forest,
Breaking through its shields of shadow,
Rushed into each secret ambush,
Searched each thicket, dingle, hollow;
Still the guests of Hiawatha
Slumbered in the silent wigwam.

From his place rose Hiawatha,
Bade farewell to old Nokomis,
Spake in whispers, spake in this wise,

Did not wake the guests, that slumbered:
　'I am going, O Nokomis,
On a long and distant journey,
To the portals of the Sunset,
To the regions of the home-wind,
Of the Northwest wind, Keewaydin.
But these guests I leave behind me,
In your watch and ward I leave them;
See that never harm comes near them,
See that never fear molests them,
Never danger nor suspicion,
Never want of food or shelter,
In the lodge of Hiawatha!'
　Forth into the village went he,
Bade farewell to all the warriors,
Bade farewell to all the young men,
Spake persuading, spake in this wise:
　'I am going, O my people,
On a long and distant journey;
Many moons and many winters
Will have come, and will have vanished
Ere I come again to see you.
But my guests I leave behind me;
Listen to their words of wisdom,
Listen to the truth they tell you,
For the Master of Life has sent them
From the land of light and morning!'
　On the shore stood Hiawatha,
Turned and waved his hand at parting;

On the clear and luminous water
Launched his birch-canoe for sailing,
From the pebbles of the margin
Shoved it forth into the water;
Whispered to it, 'Westward! westward!'
And with speed it darted forward.

And the evening sun descending
Set the clouds on fire with redness,
Burned the broad sky like a prairie,
Left upon the level water
One long track and trail of splendour,
Down whose stream, as down a river,
Westward, westward Hiawatha
Sailed into the fiery sunset,
Sailed into the purple vapours,
Sailed into the dusk of evening.

And the people from the margin
Watched him floating, rising, sinking,
Till the birch-canoe seemed lifted
High into that sea of splendour,
Till it sank into the vapours
Like the new moon slowly, slowly
Sinking in the purple distance.

And they said, 'Farewell for ever!'
Said, 'Farewell, O Hiawatha!'
And the forests, dark and lonely,
Moved through all their depths of darkness,
Sighed, 'Farewell, O Hiawatha!'
And the waves upon the margin

Rising, rippling on the pebbles,
Sobbed, 'Farewell, O Hiawatha!'
And the heron, the Shuh-shuh-gah,
From her haunts among the fenlands,
Screamed, 'Farewell, O Hiawatha!'
    Thus departed Hiawatha,
Hiawatha the Beloved,
In the glory of the sunset,
In the purple mists of evening,
To the regions of the home-wind,
Of the Northwest wind Keewaydin,
To the Islands of the Blessed,
To the kingdom of Ponemah,
To the land of the Hereafter!

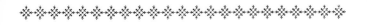

In the Churchyard at Cambridge

In the village churchyard she lies,
Dust is in her beautiful eyes,
   No more she breathes, nor feels, nor stirs;
At her feet and at her head
Lies a slave to attend the dead,
   But their dust is white as hers.

Was she a lady of high degree,
So much in love with the vanity
   And foolish pomp of this world of ours?
Or was it Christian charity,
And lowliness and humility,
   The richest and rarest of all dowers?

Who shall tell us? No one speaks;
No colour shoots into those cheeks,
   Either of anger or of pride,
At the rude question we have asked;
Nor will the mystery be unmasked
   By those who are sleeping at her side.

Hereafter? – And do you think to look
On the terrible pages of that Book
   To find her failings, faults, and errors?
Ah, you will then have other cares,
In your own shortcomings and despairs,
   In your own secret sins and terrors!

My Lost Youth

Often I think of the beautiful town
   That is seated by the sea;
Often in thought go up and down
The pleasant streets of that dear old town,
   And my youth comes back to me.
     And a verse of Lapland song
     Is haunting my memory still:
   'A boy's will is the wind's will,
And the thoughts of youth are long, long
     thoughts.'

I can see the shadowy lines of its trees,
   And catch in sudden gleams,
The sheen of the far-surrounding seas,
And the islands that were the Hesperides
   Of all my boyish dreams.
     And the burden of that old song,
     It murmurs and whispers still:
   'A boy's will is the wind's will,
And the thoughts of youth are long, long
     thoughts.'

I remember the black wharves and the slips,
   And the sea-tides tossing free;
And Spanish sailors with bearded lips,
And the beauty and mystery of the ships,
   And the magic of the sea.

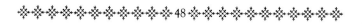

And the voice of that wayward song
   Is singing and saying still:
'A boy's will is the wind's will,
And the thoughts of youth are long, long
    thoughts.'

I remember the bulwarks by the shore,
   And the fort upon the hill;
The sunrise gun, with its hollow roar,
The drum-beat repeated o'er and o'er,
   And the bugle wild and shrill.
    And the music of that old song
    Throbs in my memory still:
'A boy's will is the wind's will,
And the thoughts of youth are long, long
    thoughts.'

I remember the sea-fight far away,
   How it thundered o'er the tide!
And the dead captains, as they lay
In their graves, o'erlooking the tranquil bay,
   Where they in battle died.
    And the sound of that mournful song
    Goes through me with a thrill:
'A boy's will is the wind's will,
And the thoughts of youth are long, long
    thoughts.'

I can see the breezy dome of groves,
    The shadows of Deering's Woods;
And the friendships old and the early loves
Come back with a sabbath sound, as of doves
    In quiet neighbourhoods.
        And the verse of that sweet old song,
            It flutters and murmurs still:
        'A boy's will is the wind's will,
And the thoughts of youth are long, long
            thoughts.'

I remember the gleams and glooms that dart
    Across the schoolboy's brain;
The song and the silence in the heart,
That in part are prophecies, and in part
    Are longings wild and vain.
        And the voice of that fitful song
            Sings on, and is never still:
        'A boy's will is the wind's will,
And the thoughts of youth are long, long
            thoughts.'

There are things of which I may not speak;
    There are dreams that cannot die;
There are thoughts that make the strong heart
        weak,
And bring a pallor into the cheek,
    And a mist before the eye.

And the words of that fatal song
   Come over me like a chill:
 'A boy's will is the wind's will,
And the thoughts of youth are long, long
     thoughts.'

Strange to me now are the forms I meet
   When I visit the dear old town;
But the native air is pure and sweet,
And the trees that o'ershadow each well-known
     street,
   As they balance up and down,
     Are singing the beautiful song,
     Are sighing and whispering still:
 'A boy's will is the wind's will,
And the thoughts of youth are long, long
     thoughts.'

And Deering's Woods are fresh and fair,
   And with joy that is almost pain
My heart goes back to wander there,
And among the dreams of the days that were,
   I find my lost youth again.
     And the strange and beautiful song,
     The groves are repeating it still:
 'A boy's will is the wind's will,
And the thoughts of youth are long, long
     thoughts.'

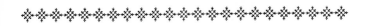

Snow-Flakes

Out of the bosom of the Air,
   Out of the cloud-folds of her garments shaken,
Over the woodlands brown and bare,
   Over the harvest fields forsaken,
     Silent, and soft, and slow
     Descends the snow.

Even as our cloudy fancies take
   Suddenly shape in some divine expression,
Even as the troubled heart doth make
   In the white countenance confession,
     The troubled sky reveals
     The grief it feels.

This is the poem of the air,
   Slowly in silent syllables recorded;
This is the secret despair,
   Long in its cloudy bosom hoarded,
     Now whispered and revealed
     To wood and field.

The Tide Rises, The Tide Falls

The tide rises, the tide falls,
The twilight darkens, the curlew calls;
Along the sea-sands damp and brown
The traveller hastens toward the town,
    And the tide rises, the tide falls.

Darkness settles on roofs and walls,
But the sea in the darkness calls and calls;
The little waves, with their soft white hands,
Efface the footprints in the sands,
    And the tide rises, the tides falls.

The morning breaks; the steeds in their stalls
Stamp and neigh, as the hostler calls;
The day returns, but nevermore
Returns the traveller to the shore,
    And the tide rises, the tide falls.

Chaucer

An old man in a lodge within a park;
    The chamber walls depicted all around
    With portraitures of huntsman, hawk, and
        hound,
    And the hurt deer. He listeneth to the lark,
Whose song comes with the sunshine through the
        dark
    Of painted glass in leaden lattice bound;
    He listeneth and he laugheth at the sound,
    Then writeth in a book like any clerk.
He is the poet of the dawn, who wrote
    The Canterbury Tales, and his old age
    Made beautiful with song; and as I read
I hear the crowing cock, I hear the note
    Of lark and linnet, and from every page
    Rise odours of ploughed field or flowery mead.

Milton

I face the sounding sea-beach and behold
    How the voluminous billows roll and run,
    Upheaving and subsiding, while the sun
    Shines through their sheeted emerald far
        unrolled,
And the ninth wave, slow gathering fold by fold
    All its loose-flowing garments into one,
    Plunges upon the shore, and floods the dun
    Pale reach of sands, and changes them to gold.
So in majestic cadence rise and fall
    The mighty undulations of thy song,
    O sightless bard, England's Mæonides!
And ever and anon, high over all
    Uplifted, a ninth wave superb and strong,
    Floods all the soul with its melodious seas.

Killed at the Ford

He is dead, the beautiful youth,
The heart of honour, the tongue of truth,
He, the life and light of us all,
Whose voice was blithe as a bugle-call,
Whom all eyes followed with one consent,
The cheer of whose laugh, and whose pleasant
    word,
Hushed all murmurs of discontent.

Only last night, as we rode along,
Down the dark of the mountain gap,
To visit the picket-guard at the ford,
Little dreaming of any mishap,
He was humming the words of some old song:
'Two red roses he had on his cap,
And another he bore at the point of his sword.'

Sudden and swift a whistling ball
Came out of a wood, and the voice was still;
Something I heard in the darkness fall,
And for a moment my blood grew chill;
I spake in a whisper, as he who speaks
In a room where some one is lying dead;
But he made no answer to what I said.

We lifted him up to his saddle again,
And through the mire and the mist and the rain
Carried him back to the silent camp,
And laid him as if asleep on his bed;
And I saw by the light of the surgeon's lamp
Two white roses upon his cheeks,
And one, just over his heart, blood-red!

And I saw in a vision how far and fleet
That fatal bullet went speeding forth,
Till it reached a town in the distant North,
Till it reached a house in a sunny street,
Till it reached a heart that ceased to beat
Without a murmur, without a cry;
And a bell was tolled, in that far-off town,
For one who had passed from cross to crown,
And the neighbours wondered that she should die.

NOTES ON THE PICTURES

p. 6   *Falls of the Kaaterskill*, 1826, by Thomas Cole. Reproduced by courtesy of the Warner Collection of Gulf States Paper Corporation, Tuscaloosa, Alabama.

p. 15   *Shipwreck* (detail), by Siegwald Johannes (1827–1902). In the collection of Rasmus Mayer, Bergen, Norway. Photo ET Archive, London.

p. 19   *Shoeing,* exh. 1844, by Sir Edwin Landseer. Reproduced by courtesy of the Trustees of the Tate Gallery, London.

p. 22   *The Precipice, c.* 1827, by Francis Danby. Reproduced by courtesy of the City of Bristol Museum and Art Gallery, England.

p. 26   *A Ride for Liberty – The Fugitive Slaves, c.* 1862, by Eastman Johnson. Reproduced by courtesy of The Brooklyn Museum, New York. Gift of Miss Gwendolyn O. L. Conkling.

p. 30   *West Point, Prout's Neck,* 1900, by Winslow Homer. Reproduced by courtesy of the Sterling and Francine Clark Art Institute, Williamstown, Massachusetts.

p. 34   *Independence* (Squire Jack Porter), 1858, by Frank Blackwell Mayer. Reproduced by courtesy of the National Museum of American Art, Smithsonian Institution, Washington, DC. Harriet Lane Johnston Collection.

p. 39   *Buffalo Bull's Back Fat, Head Chief, Blood Tribe,* 1832, by George Catlin. Reproduced by courtesy of the National Museum of American Art, Smithsonian Institution, Washington, DC. Gift of Mrs Joseph Harrison, Jr.

p. 51   *Lovers of the Sun,* by Henry Scott Tuke (1858–1929). In the Forbes Magazine Collection, New York. Photo Bridgeman Art Library, London.

p. 55   *Meditation by the Sea, c.* 1850–60, Anonymous. Reproduced by courtesy of the Museum of Fine Arts, Boston. M. and M. Karolik Collection.

p. 59   *The Mountain Ford,* 1846, by Thomas Cole. Reproduced by courtesy of the Metropolitan Museum of Art, New York. Bequest of Maria DeWitt Jessup from the collection of her husband Morris K. Jessup.

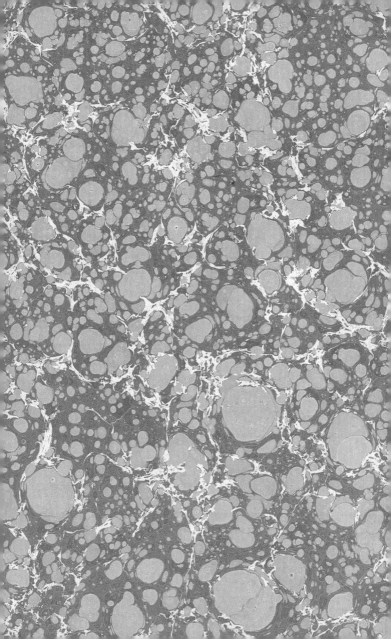